Anne Odeke, Guleraana Mir,
Kenny Emson and Sadie Hasler

Misfits

Salamander Street

PLAYS

First published in 2020 by Salamander Street Ltd.
(info@salamanderstreet.com)

ISBN: 9781913630904

Printed and bound in Great Britain

10 9 8 7 6 5 4 3 2 1

QUEEN'S THEATRE HORNCHURCH

Queen's Theatre Hornchurch (QTH) is a vibrant producing theatre, working in Outer East London, Essex and beyond. As a cultural hub, over 210,000 people enjoy the programme each year. Audiences are guaranteed a warm welcome from a three year winner of UK Theatre's Most Welcoming Theatre (2016 – 2018) and London Theatre of the Year 2020 (The Stage Awards), the first Outer London theatre to receive this prestigious award.

Since the appointment of Douglas Rintoul as Artistic Director and Mathew Russell as Executive Director, productions have included the record breaking regional premiere of *Priscilla, Queen of the Desert*, and critically acclaimed regional premieres of musicals *Made in Dagenham* and *Once,* both co-produced with the New Wolsey Ipswich. QTH world premiered a commissioned adaptation of *The Invisible Man* by Clem Garritty and *Abi* by Atiha Sen Gupta, co-produced with Derby Theatre.

Productions are seen on tour by more than 40,000 people each year. *The Crucible,* co-produced with Selladoor Productions, undertook a five month tour, a major revival of *Kindertransport* was produced in an innovative international partnership with Les Theatre de la Ville de Luxembourg, *Abigail's Party* was co-produced with Derby Theatre and Salisbury Playhouse, and the musical *The Hired Man* with Hull Truck Theatre and Oldham Coliseum.

QTH is at the **heart of the local community**, and offers a wide range of life enhancing workshops and classes for people of all ages – working with more than 34,000 participants last year. QTH was Theatre partner to the National Theatre for **Public Acts**, a new landmark initiative to create extraordinary acts of theatre and community, producing the European premiere of the musical adaptation of *As You Like It*, which saw 149 participants from across London's diverse communities experiencing a life changing performance on QTH's stage.

QTH talent development programme, *Outer Limits,* connects with local and regional professional artists, offering essential support that hasn't previously existed. **Essex on Stage** is an ambitious programme led by QTH, championing positive notions of Essex, and celebrating theatre made by working-class people, made possible by the Theatre receiving the **2018 Clothworkers' Foundation Theatre Award**. This was launched with the regional premiere of David Eldridge's *In Basildon* and an ambitious rep season, offering the world premiere of Sadie Hasler's *Stiletto Beach* and London premiere of Luke Norris' *So Here We Are*.

Situated in the borough with the 4th lowest arts engagement in London, QTH has led a successful consortium bid for £1 million of new Creative People and Places funding, towards Havering Changing, a partnership seeking radical new ideas to engage local communities in arts and culture. Last year, an astonishing 45% of QTH's audience were new to the Theatre.

Havering LONDON BOROUGH

Supported using public funding by
ARTS COUNCIL ENGLAND

ESSEX ON STAGE

Essex on Stage is an ambitious new two-year programme led by Queen's Theatre Hornchurch, championing positive notions of Essex, celebrating theatre made by working-class people and raising aspirations for emerging artists from Essex and Outer East London. It includes commissioning new plays, establishing a network of venues, touring drama about Essex across Essex for new audiences, organising local events to develop talent and making life-changing projects with communities.

Essex on Stage has been made possible by the generous support of The Clothworkers' Foundation. Queen's Theatre Hornchurch is the recipient of the 2018 Clothworkers' Theatre Award, a competitive annual prize given to a regional producing theatre, that has only ever been awarded five times.

THE CLOTHWORKERS' FOUNDATION

The Clothworkers' Theatre Award was part of a broader five year £1.25million programme to support the dramatic arts, which saw The Clothworkers' Foundation awarded annual funds of £150,000 to five venues across the UK Theatre membership between 2014 and 2018.

The annual award was given to a regional producing theatre in England. The prize could be used for anything from capital works to sponsoring a touring production. It must be used for the specific purpose stated in the theatre's application and not added to the theatre's general funds.

In selecting the winner of the award, the Clothworkers' Foundation took into account factors such as the theatre's recent achievements, and the strength of the project proposal including the impact it hopes to make.

Last Lockdown, in the swirling madness of Covid, while all the theatres were closed, Queen's Theatre Hornchurch determined in their eminent 'sod this for a game of soldiers' wisdom, to commission new work. They brought together four working-class playwrights from Essex to write four interwoven monologues; to tell a story of Epic Essex; of identity, & resilience.

Kenny, Anne, Guleraana & I were staggered to be commissioned to write anything at all during such an historic & troubling time for theatre.

We met for writers meetings on Zoom – the new way of life – we pondered ideas, went away & wrote, & rewrote, & rewrote. Chatted with Doug, a lot. Then rewrote some more.

We wrote big bold personal words from the heart; barked out our guts. We stuck big sharp shards from our lives & imaginations into a strange amalgam of what it means to be 'from Essex'. That famous county known all over the globe for 'just being so Essex'. As though people not from here can know what that means; really means.

Months later, *Misfits* is a big beast with a fiercely beating heart; angry, loving, funny, & very real.

As we go into Lockdown 2 – as these words go into print, while we nervously wait for US election results to be declared, a quiet Christmas, and all the uncertainty that lies beyond this new period of isolation – restrictions mean that we can't share those words live in the theatre every night.

But we can in fact go bigger, wider, and share it — our Essex — with the world. And while nightly live-streaming is not theatre as we've known it, it is new and exciting and we're incredibly lucky to be making work when so many can't. This has to be a brave new world, and we need humans and stories, collaboration & togetherness, more than ever.

We hope you enjoy the company of Daisy, Fiza, Tag & Princess Dinubolu. They have so much to tell you. ❤

Sadie, Kenny, Guleraana, & Anne

***

For Doug, Mathew — and all at Queen's. With love and thanks from four very grateful writers, now and always. You are the best of Essex.

And big love to the real people stitched into these stories. x

Misfits by Anne Odeke, Guleraana Mir, Kenny Emson and Sadie Hasler was first performed on 11 November 2020, in a production live streamed from the theatre.

Co-Director **Douglas Rintoul**
Co-Director **Emma Baggott**
Lighting Designer **Stephen Pemble**
Sound Designer **Adrienne Quartly**
Video Designer **Daniel Denton**
Videographer **Chris Faulkner**
Costume Supervisor **Nicola Thomas**
Executive Producer **Mathew Russell**

Head of Production **Christine Piper**
Company Stage Manager **Lauren Harvey-Dempster**
Deputy Stage Manager **Sarah Jenkins**
Assistant Stage Manager **Daniel Haynes**
Sound Operator **Michael Bennett**
Technician **Josh Mead**

Cast

EUNICE/JOANNA **Anne Odeke**
DAISY **Gemma Salter**
FIZA **Mona Goodwin**
TAG (RICHARD) **Thomas Coombes**

A relatively empty stage. There is a bar stool, a bench that could be in a school or a church, a plastic hospital chair, a microphone on a stand and a mannequin with an early 20ᵗʰ Century red dress on it. There are two boxes, one large and one small. Both are reinforced so the characters can sit or stand on them.

PROLOGUE

There's a fast-paced montage of sound and visuals from the characters' lives. It crescendos then suspends to reveal **DAISY**, **EUNICE**, **FIZA**, *and* **TAG** *in spotlights on the four corners of the stage.*

It's just when I think about it…

The first thing…

The first thing that comes into my mind…

It's…

Towie

Chavs

Essex Girls

Fake tan

Lager,

Lager,

Lager,

Lager,

Shouting.

Lager,

Lager,

Lager,

Lager,

Shouting

Mega mega white thing, mega mega white –

Where are you from?

Originally?

Stanford – le – Hope

The London Borough of Havering

Southend

Leigh. On fucking sea.

You mean Hornchurch, right?

Sounds posh.

The airport?

On the estuary?

Nah, mate.

Not. At. All.

Essex.

My Essex.

The sounds and visuals gather speed underscored by the buzzing of a fluorescent tube light growing in volume that cuts abruptly like a switch revealing **DAISY** *alone on stage leaning on a hospital chair centre stage looking at the audience.*

SCENE 1

The distant sound of an ambulance.

DAISY: I just bloody walked here. Which I think might have been the worst decision I ever made. But I didn't want to just wait at home because I'm not sure what I'm meant to be waiting for. Apart from a baby. *(She gestures to her tummy.)*

Obviously. Even with the NCT, the Hypnobirthing classes, and the constant googling, I'm still not really sure what to expect from this. Labour. Birth. The rest of my life really.

I've been plonked in a different country with no map, and a blindfold on. And I'm being told to get to the town centre. But I don't know where the town centre is. Because I don't know what country I'm in. Anyway. You get the picture.

I've given up on my dream of going to the toilet and the baby just falling out. I think that's probably not going to happen now if I'm honest.

DAISY has a flicker of nervousness and picks up her phone. Stares at the screen.

I should've phoned Mum. She made me promise I'd call when the time came, but I just…

She's not ready to go there yet.

So I've been doing these hypnobirthing classes, because I really like the thought of doing this the natural way? The group is so nice. They made me feel so comfortable not having the Dad there. Coz I really want to feel empowered in all this, you know? That was important to me. A little bit Up Yours Patriarchy, lone-wolf danger-mama. You know?

DAISY's in the circle at Hypnobirthing.

Hi, I'm Daisy. Erm. I'm due in March. I'm having a girl. Really happy about that. Not that it matters as long as it's healthy. But, you know. Yay girls. *(She bashfully pats her tummy proudly.)* Erm…I've read a lot about hypnobirthing and it just sounds really nice? So here I am.

She grimaces as there's another surge. Then she's back. Chair returned to its usual position.

It's hard when everyone in the group is so different to you. Couples. With houses. Mortgages. Serious careers. Pensions. Insurance. Spare car. So sorted, so happy. They've got armour, you know? For the future. They talk about life so casually, like it's not something they have to figure out from day to day, and all I could think was 'That's not normal, is it, all that? Have I missed something *massive*?

I didn't like to mention the fact I'd moved home twenty-three times and most of those were two bedroom flats, apart from the *one* bedroom flats, and that one bedsit in York Road between Stabby Central and the Polish brothel, opposite the crack den, where I hid watching Netflix for three months after a break-up, before I realised I wanted to stay alive actually, and moved out – funny what makes you realise you like living. So yeah, I didn't like to mention I'd just moved from a one bedroom flat into a two bedroom flat and hadn't even painted the second bedroom all nice for a baby yet. So I just drifted off. Thought about the cheeky burger I was going to get on the way home.

DAISY's *at the Drive-Thru Maccy D's. Music blares out of her car. The order hatch lights up her face like a beacon of yellow joy. On the screen: those celestial yellow arches. She turns her music down to speak.*

Oh hiya. Can I just get a double cheeseburger please?

Is that everything?

Um. Yeah, so, two of those. *(Beat.)* And large fries.

D'you wanna make that a meal?

Okay, yeah, make those meals. One with a chocolate milkshake. And one…with an orange juice. *(She strokes her tummy. Then, to baby…)* That's for you.

You can drive to the next window now. Enjoy your meal.

Thank you. We will.

I comforted myself that almost the entire population of Manhattan lives in flats and that Manhattan is dead cool. No one in New York can afford a house unless you're some Trump loving psychopath on the Forbes list. And no one has a garden so their dogs have to piss in Central Park, and their kids have to play b'ball outside of the school and stuff. It's a massive social equaliser. But Southend is not Manhattan. If Manhattan is the Big Apple, Southend is the shrivelled old satsuma you find under the sofa.

People think of Southend as this slightly scummy embarrassment – one big housing estate attached to some arcades where everyone goes round pissed and poor and robbing each other. And obviously there is some of that. But there's also insane money in Southend. I don't think I'd really noticed it before. But being a single woman with a baby growing inside her gets you noticing all the stuff you haven't got.

I've always seen myself as somewhere in the middle, nowhere near poor but nowhere near posh either. I liked my life. I felt free. But, you could definitely say that in being so free I was also at a distinct disadvantage compared to everyone else in my group.

I certainly never told them I've been pregnant before. Twice. I keep those secrets pressed tight to my chest. Twice I'd held a match and watched the flame flicker – before blowing it out. Not the right time. I wasn't ready. Wasn't right. Wasn't perfect.

I had all this ringing in my guts as I sat in a plastic chair which squeaked like a parrot fart and stared at the Doctor's gold cross and told her what I wanted. What I thought I wanted. She didn't say anything. And then she asked if I was sure. I squared up to Medicine & Faith and tried to remember I am my own woman with the right to choose. I said... 'yeah'.

Medicine and Faith stared me down; bored through my eyes, down my tubes and through membranes and slop and muscular mechanics, past the heart, like a sloppy clock, ticktock ticktock, down to it. To what would be her. The doctor said

If you do this again please don't come to me, see someone else.

Thud. That sinks in.

I didn't feel the rage til later.

She took the form fresh from the printer. I watched her sign it. Stared at the white crescent moons of her nails on her smooth brown hands. And a little voice said, 'when are you going to let yourself love?' I thought shut up. And it said, 'no, when are you going to let yourself love?' I stood and took the form and I went to the door and said

'Thank you.'

The doctor kept her eyes on her screen and I left. And all day I heard that little voice

Like a heartbeat…

When. Are you going. To let. Yourself.

Love.

I never phoned the number on the form. At some point I realised – it wasn't ever going to be perfect. Life isn't perfect. Maybe I didn't deserve it. Maybe those two big secrets of mine were jinxing me. Maybe I needed to break the curse. Do something big and mad and bold and maybe beautiful.

That's when I decided to keep it. Her. But I kept the Doctor's note folded up in my purse. It's still there.

I was halfway through painting one wall of the nursery – a.k.a. the box room, just big enough for the cot and me to stand beside it, *just* – when I had my first contraction. Thought it was a period pain, then half an hour later I remembered I don't have periods anymore, and that it might be the baby saying 'strap in mama'.

I thought back to that day, that cubicle, at school, aged thirteen in the year 9 loos. Something felt a bit wet. Blood. The tiny riot of seeing that, just sat there on the loo, silent but changed forever.

And I put some loo roll in my knickers & walked home so carefully, bearing that little secret like a royal baby. I went home and I told Mum.

Muuuum.

That long drawn out mum. That build up mum. Muuum, can I go to Vicki's after I've done my homework. Muuuum, can I have a lift. Muuum, can I watch Dirty Dancing. Muuum, I went to the loo and I saw… blood – in my knickers and…

And it's such a small moment. So clumsy and small and dull. Now I'd probably shout: I AM WOMAN. I BLEED. I AM FERTILE AS AMAZONIAN SOIL. SEW YOUR SEED IN ME AND I SHALL BEAR INCREDIBLE TREES OF SUCH LUSTROUS FRUIT, YOU SHALL WEEP AT THE WOMANHOOD I WIELD, while beating my breasts or something. But I just said 'I think I've started my period.'

And waited for mum to tell me it was okay.

I felt so proud. This is it, Mum. I bleed. I'm just like you.

Then every month like clockwork, you start to spot the signs. So later you know when something's wrong. You can feel when it's different. Late. When you might be…

I've never been early for anything in my life. In fact I've been constantly, characteristically late. Late to the pub, late to films (always miss the trailers), late to the party, (straight to the kitchen with tequila), late to find a job I like, late to love, (so many mistakes), late to have a baby.

EUNICE *enters and sits on the bench upstage centre.*

But I never *felt* late. I never felt like I was chasing anything. Rushing. Catching up. And then all of a sudden I realised I'm way nearer forty than thirty and I've got…

…nothing. Suddenly everything I loved felt like it's not enough. I've been dancing down a dead-end street. Still renting. Still floating between jobs like a freelance turd. Still going to the pub three times a week. Still eating out. Still fanny-arsing about with men I know aren't right. Dating.

There's a growing sound of applause as **EUNICE** *stands up and hesitantly walks forward to downstage centre over the following dialogue.*

Because sod getting into anything serious with someone who isn't right, right? Especially when I've been through so much, healed so often, picked myself up again and again, right? But it's all fine because I've got time. I've still got so much time. Right?

SCENE 2

October. Modern Day. Assembly. The hall of a Christian secondary school in Essex. It's Black History Month. **EUNICE** *is fifteen and stands holding her speech. She looks tense.*

EUNICE: No, thank **you** Mrs Bates, and thank **you** Year 10. I would like to begin by saying to you all how honoured and touched I was, to be invited by our Deputy Head to speak to you all this morning about a topic that is very close to <u>my</u> heart, and I'm sure, very close to the heart of many of you sitting here today.

DAISY *on not getting an answer leaves the stage.*

We know from our History lessons that we very rarely get to speak about Black History – I have studied the Tudors three times – No jokes.

You may ask yourself then, 'Where are all the black people?' Well, I say to you – that is a very excellent question, and this is why each year during the month of October we mark *Black History Month*; a month in which we are encouraged to celebrate the achievements of Black people throughout history.

For ages, and I do mean like *ages*, I thought about what I could talk to you about this morning since history is obviously quite big, and I decided, since we're in Shoebury, that I should share with you all a bit about Black Essex History. So, basically, I Googled it, and I found after numerous searches; *'Black Essex History'*, *'Black people Essex History'*, *'History of Essex Black people'*, *'Black Essex persons in time'*, *'Historically important Black Essex Folk'*, *'Tudor slash Georgian slash Jacobean slash Victorian Black Essex people'*, that it basically turns out, there's a lot on The **Black Death** – which of course in this moment isn't very helpful to us. Neither was *Essex witches and the art of **Black Magic*** – that kept coming up and being honest, that did just lead me down a very dark hole. Apparently, there's a lovely pub in Maldon called the ***Black Rabbit*** – that actually looked nice. Then quite a bit more about the **Black Death** until eventually, *(Excitedly.)* I did find something!

The Windrush Generation; You know, the Caribbean people? Their ships docked at Tilbury. *(EUNICE doesn't get the response she quite expected and so continues.)* Soooooo, what that means is that the Windrush Generations first ever steps on British soil, was actually Essex soil. Like, that is huuuuuge.

(Excitedly remembering.) I also found a sentence about how the first **ever** recorded Black person in Essex was a guy called 'Thomas Parker' and that was in 1580 – and yes, that is literally all we know about him, *but* it means that Black people have been definitely been in our county for nearly 450 years – I know, right?!

(Even more excited.) **Then**, I found this tiny, like I mean *tiny* mention of a black woman in 1908 – a black *Essex* woman from Southend-on-Sea *(Pause.)*. Like, I'm not being funny or nothing, but that is where I was born; Southend Hospital; that is also where my Mum works. This woman and I have probably stood in the same places, walked the same streets, sat under the same tree.

She was incredible – or incredibly stupid depending on your point of view.

(Thinking) You see, being honest, there are times when say, I'm at the chippy, or in ASDA, that I look around – I look around and…

I aint' finished! You – you told me I had ten minutes. I ain't even got to the best bit. Ten minutes you said. No, you '*Sit down please*', two more minutes then? Why?!

EUNICE *tries to talk over the interruption. At the same time* **FIZA** *enters 'Cardigan' by Taylor Swift plays – at first very faint and full of reverb.* **FIZA** *takes her place amongst the boxes. This is her childhood bedroom. The music grows as* **EUNICE** *picks up what was* **DAISY**'s *chair and defends herself with it. She is then chased off stage.* **FIZA** *is on the ground, arms and legs outstretched, sort of like she's making a snow angel, and she lets the music seep in. She feels the song deeply. It's upsetting and triggering, yet almost validating. She sits up and sways, signing along to every other word. She might be compelled to get up and dance with an imaginary partner; maybe a hoodie that's lying on the side is used to represent that partner? Maybe she's just so fucking emo she sits and stares at the audience as tears stream down her face.*

SCENE 3

As the song ends **FIZA** *immediately goes to play it again. It restarts. A deep sigh, she's not done wallowing AT ALL. But then she clocks the audience and the music screeches off. Fuck! This is embarrassing!*

FIZA: I'm sorry but sometimes I restart a song before I've even got to the end of it, I need it that bad. Count yourself lucky that you only had to sit through it once. Could have been much worse.

The lyric video for Cardigan by Taylor Swift is shot from above. Yes I watched it, repeatedly, for about ninety minutes straight. That was the longest –

In the video we are looking down on a shoreline. Waves ebb and flow at a fairly regular pace. Just out of frame there are rocks. The waves crash on them with enough force to create that white foamy stuff – seafoam. I imagine the perspective is that of a woman standing at the edge of a cliff, looking down, contemplating. She wears a dress. Her hair loose and scraggly at the ends hangs over her shoulders. She's thinking about what it would take to…

I don't know when I went from Courtney Love to Taylor Swift either.

Returning to live in my childhood bedroom has certainly contributed. But there's a part of me that thinks it was a slow decline; a snail-paced draining of self. Like I left the tap on juuuuust a smidge and everything I loved about myself dripped out onto the floor of our marital home.

That judgement is based on the assumption that Taylor Swift is less than Courtney Love…and there's a right, or a wrong way to be a rock star, or a feminist role model. I think maybe I'm a mix of them both? But what do I know? I have a profoundly inept sense of self.

ALEXA *chimes a reminder notification.*

ALEXA: I'm reminding you to RSVP to the reunion.

She ignores it, embarrassed. **ALEXA** *continues.*

I'm reminding you to RSVP to the reunion.

FIZA: Alexa! Not right now, we have company.

ALEXA: I'm reminding you to RSVP to the reunion.

ALEXA *chimes, about to remind* **FIZA** *again.*

FIZA:	ALEXA! Snooze!
ALEXA:	Reminder snoozed.
FIZA:	In a few months it will have been twenty years since I left secondary school. Someone has decided to hold a reunion. *Someone* is obviously doing really well in life.
	Not that long ago I was also doing well, I also wanted to show off. Now I – I don't know what the point is. Morbid curiosity – wanting to see what everyone else is up to? There's always someone worse off than you. Does that make me a vampire? Building myself up at the expense of others.
	Could it maybe, possibly be fun? A new beginning?

Her phone pings. She goes to read the notification.

Confession. I've signed up to OKCupid.

These things didn't exist the last time I was single. The last time I was single Facebook barely existed. We didn't have emojis, or gifs, or – Unsolicited dick pics were the stuff of dreams! I know how to use the internet. Just not like this. I *have* watched almost every episode of Catfish though, so I think I've got *that* aspect of online dating sorted. Got a list of warning signs, a chart of potential red flags etc.

It's the whole making a profile bit I can't get my head around. I feel silly but it's asking me for my current location. What a loaded question!

She types and then deletes.

No. Not that.

She types –

That sounds wanky.

Untypes.

I want to be profound.

A look. That was peak wanky.

I can't fill in a dating profile! I have no idea who I am right now, newly single at thirty-seven years old. Who is this person with only a bed and two boxes to their name?

*The large box glows, surprising **FIZA**. She goes to investigate. It's mesmerising.*

What was so special that I packed it away and left it to rot in this place? Is it better or worse than the one I brought back with me, full of failure?

*The smaller box glows in response to her mentioning it. They both glow alternately, in competition with each other, demanding attention. A hectic amount of bass can be heard. The earth beneath the audience's feet should vibrate. **TAG** enters and takes his place stage right on the bar stool.*

Only one way to find out.

FIZA *hesitates, and then chooses. She opens the box. It stops as suddenly as it started.*

SCENE 4

TAG: I know what you're thinking.

Yes. This is an IPA.

My drink of choice now. Like a bit of flavour. The hops. Less gassy than lager. Less synthetic.

FIZA *sits next to the box.*

I drank Nelson Mandela for the first nineteen years of my life. Stella Artois, reassuringly expensive. I say nineteen years, I really mean the few between getting pissed up the park and my nineteenth birthday. That's when I got the fuck out of Dodge. Or to be more precise, Essex. My home. The county of my birth. And when I say Essex I mean real Essex too. Not that North Essex, quasi Suffolk village shite, people from Colchester talk about.

I mean the Shell refineries. Tilbury Docks. Corringham Town Centre Park with its burnt out swings. The ten-foot graffiti on the underpass as you come into town that tells you:

Steve Buck is a Grass.

And he was.

Thurrock. Lakeside. The Circus Tavern. Romford. Baz Vegas. Southend. The Front.

The Front.

A moment.

My dad used to call it man wine, IPA.

Want another pint of man wine, boy?

Yes, Dad.

Want a flake in it?

No, Dad.

You sure?

I'm sure.

You sure, you're sure.

Yes, I'm fucking –

Never stopped taking the piss my old man. Not till he carked it. And even then he went out with a smile on his face. Like he'd farted and no one in the room knew who it was. Fair play to him. Life and soul. Worked hard. A grafter. One of those people that everyone calls a racist now coz he voted for Brexit. That all my educated friends sat around me post about on their Facebook and Twitter. Describe him like he's another species.

And that's on my mind right now.

It's on my mind coz I know my old man wouldn't have lasted ten minutes in a boozer like this. We're in one of those hipster type bars. It's Manchester. The Northern Quarter. But it could be anywhere. People wear hats inside. People fake laugh at other people's fake stories. People pay six quid for a scotch egg. And people drink IPA.

He takes another sip of his pint.

Someone wanders over to the jukebox. I don't think anyone in here thought it actually worked. Just a prop. Just something to try and make this look more like a pub than a waiting room for some upmarket dentist.

I'm ready for some Oxbridge guitar band whining about climate change. I'm ready for –

Richard, are you listening?

I get dragged back to the conversation. Talk of mortgages. Kids. Targets at work. Twitter arguments. Brexit. Politics. Filler. Fucking mastic.

When did life just become mastic?

How the fuck did I end up here?

How the fuck did I end up in a room with these people?

How the fuck did this become my life?

But the record saves me from this moment of introspection.

The first few bars of Shy FX and UK Apachi's 'Original Nuttah' start to play.

And I feel my feet start to move. An unconscious action. Reflex. Then my hands come up to around my chin. Just like they always used to. Just like…

And I can't stop it. I can't stop that feeling. And the people I'm with are starting to look at me weird.

23

Embarrassed. Some of them are giving it that kind of '*Is this meant to be ironic?*' look. The one people like them do. But this is the least ironic thing that has ever happened.

And there's this thing building up in my throat. Not my throat. My stomach. Not my stomach. My soul. My fucking soul. Like some kind of primal feeling. And I'm trying to push it down. I'm trying to be this nice office working cunt, out with his posh mates. The one who barely calls home. The one who fell out of touch with all of his old mates. His best mates. His lie down in front of traffic for him mates. But I can't. I can't…
ESSSSSSSSSSSSSSSSSSSSSSSSSSSSSSSSSSSSSSSSSSSSSS SSSSSEX!

The bassline kicks in. It should be INSANELY LOUD.

TAG *starts to dance. It's completely carefree. Limbs are flying around. He literally doesn't give a fuck. It should be as joyful to watch as it is for him to experience. He sings along, getting some words wrong and some words right. It doesn't matter.*

We find **FIZA** *a few moments before we left her, just about to open the box.*

> And I'm back there.
> I'm nineteen.
> I'm…

As FIZA opens the box, one of the shittest songs in the world plays – 'Last Resort' by Papa Roach. **FIZA** *closes the box as quickly as possible. The music stops.*

SCENE 5

FIZA: You heard that too? *(To audience.)*

FIZA *opens the box again, this time the music floods the room. Shut. What the actual fuck is going on? She looks around her room to see if there's some sort of gadget operating this. There's not. She can't work it out.*

> Are you doing that? No? Really? Have I [finally lost it?]

Grabbing her duvet as a literal safety blanket she approaches again and ever so slowly opens the box. This time 'I Want You Bad' by The Offspring plays. She prefers this song and so stands and listens to it. Her head starts bobbing in time to the beat, she's almost enjoying it.

When the music suddenly changes to 'Beating Heart Baby' by Head Automatica, she's intrigued and sticks her head in. A memory pours out. It is bright and loud and full of wonder. Throwing off the duvet she begins to dance, jumping up and down.

ALL: Girl you gotta get away from me. Cause yooooooo want nothing to do with me. Baby is this love for real? Let me in your arms for *(they all make a sound because no one actually knows what this lyric is)*. The beating of your heart baby!

The music changes. 'Hella Good' by No Doubt. Cheers. **FIZA***'s realised where she is.*

FIZA: Pacific Edge! Friday night! Alternative night, our night. One half of my mates are upstairs, head banging. The other are downstairs wearing dresses over jeans, shaking their shoulders in time to Last Night by The Strokes.

                We came here every Friday night. I never knew where I wanted to be. I'd spend the night running up down the stairs trying to catch the best of both rooms, best of a disparate and varied friends group.

A pint of snakebite appears. She takes it.

                Ermahgod what? Snakebite?!

The music snaps to 'My Own Worst Enemy' by Lit. The others melt away. Suddenly the air is different. Cool and full of promise. She sniffs…the smell reminds her of something.

                End of the night burger van! A celebration in itself. Someone's ordered me an egg and pineapple.

A burger wrapped in paper appears. She stares at it, this is too much!

                I don't even care that I'm allergic to pineapple because I'm too busy watching people doing cartwheels up and down the marketplace. My heart beats perfectly in time with the thundering bass of the music pouring out of the club.

The faint sound of bass.

Heat in my chest, on my cheeks. Clammy hands. The urge to cheer. What is this?

She cartwheels. She stands face to the sky, arms up and breathes deeply. The beat we can hear in the background slowly morphs into 'Sale of the Century' by Sleeper.

Before Pacific Edge there was Hollywoods on a Monday night. Sticky floors and underage patrons. Then RM1 on Friday where the sweat dripped off the walls, but we bathed in it because we were eighteen and (finally) legal. I was going through a sober phase and spent my nights developing a heart arrhythmia knocking back cans of red bull.

Later, Thursdays at Opium Lounge. At one point there was an alternative night out for almost each day of the week, which in a world dominated by Time & Envy, drum and bass music and impenetrable social hierarchies, felt massive. Suddenly walking down the high street felt like the right kind of dangerous.

We began to occupy the same big window seat in the Moon & Stars in Romford every Friday night. The one by the stairs to the toilets. I started to recognise the other patrons week after week, and it felt iconic. The day someone referred to us as locals I glowed from the inside out. Suburban achievement unlocked.

She celebrates.

I went into what used to be Pacific Edge. It serves brunch. Brunch! I like brunch! Brunch is not what I would have expected. But then I suppose places are allowed to change, unlike people.

Am I the version of me that used to jump up and down to songs in fishnets, or the me that now only wants their eggs poached?

We hear the congregation sing 'Lord dismiss us with thy blessing'. **JOANNA** *enters and sits on her pew a little down centre stage.*

SCENE 6

June 1908. A church in Southend-on-Sea. **JOANNA** *is getting herself in a bit of a tizz as she chats to God.*

JOANNA: I try my best – I was brought up that way you see. Mary and me, we've our Father to thank for that – he was 'Godly', well, he wasn't always – it was only when he come over to here from Uganda that he thought he should make an effort to *blend* in. FYI it's 1908.

(She stands and makes a sign of the cross.) I come here every Sunday, and I can't see a thing. Not just because the priest has his back to us, but each week, I'm forced to sit so close to the exit *(Gesturing just behind her.)*, that I might as well be sat in the pub – no jokes.

(Confessing.) I come 'ere because it's important for people to know that I come; that I am a *good* person – dya see? *(Spotting them.)* You'll notice that the family I work for have got front row seats – that's because the more money you have, the closer you are to God, and these folk are completely minted.

(Shaking her head.) To me, that just don't make no sense – I don't mean any disrespect, but weren't Jesus even, like *me*? You know, someone with no money? An outcast? Brown?? I mean, what dya reckon he'd say? I'd say ask him, but I bet he's busy.

Why is it that 'status' is **everything**? You can be dark skinned; a Negro, Indian, Chinese, Middle Eastern, have one leg, four ears, a tail even, but so long as you have money and/or a title, you are deemed important. *(Pointing to herself.)* Money – no, Coloured – yes, Married – No, British – Yes, but it don't matter that I was born here – I'm invisible.

The hymn ends. **JOANNA** *sits*

Mrs Appleby *saw* me earlier. I was 'in her way' as I was
waiting to enter a pew. She told me that if people like me
wish to *'play white'* and come to church, they should dress
accordingly and not *'Like a savage'* – she then pointed at
my hair.

Funny, how the Empire reached out to *'savages'* to help
win the Boer War.

(Becoming angry.) Even when leaving the Church there are
certain social politics at play. Why is it always that the
people at the front leave first? This has never made sense
to me because *(again)* I'm literally right by the door, but
then perhaps you think that us folk need more time in
here? It's all part of *the game*. And the game, for people
like me, never changes. Nothing changes. We'll all still be
here next year, and the year after, and the year after that
– still praying, still sitting at the back, still having to hold
our tongue.

(The sound of altar bells.)

Reverend Howard's announcing the parish notices.
'The Banns of Marriage…' – They make a really cute
couple. *'Still needing a volunteer to man the Milk Churn stall
at the Summer fete'* – no thanks, and now, *'…a little against
Church etiquette'* (?) – *sounds interesting.* He's licking his lips
– Whatever it is, he's making me nervous. He's pointing
at Mr Bacon, the supervisor at The Kursaal. Mr Bacon
has begged him to make us aware that there are only
a handful of places left for his beauty pageant next
month, and should any of the young ladies within our
congregation be interested, they should get in touch with
him immediately. Not only will the winner be crowned
Miss Southend, but they'll also receive a small cash prize
and have their picture in the local paper. Would any
ladies be interested? Any at all?

Strip lights flicker. **DAISY** *switches into severe pain. She gets up, paces the floor, shifting into strange positions, jutting her bum out and resting against the bed as she tries to get "comfortable".*

> *(Mumbling under her breath.)* Mrs Fraser's twin daughters' are suddenly sitting upright. *(With raised eyebrows until she realises who it is.)* Behind me there's whispering… It's Adele. She's twelve – she looks just like me when I was her age. Her mother's saying something…*whispering* something, *"Don't…be…so stupid. This ain't…for…people like us. Do you know…what would happen to you…if you put your hand up?"*

DAISY *returns to her hospital chair and she's fumbling with her mobile phone. There's that buzzing of the fluorescent lights again.* **JOANNA** *turns to Adele, then the Vicar, then back to Adele, then the Vicar. Suddenly* **JOANNA** *raises her hand above her head.* **DAISY** *simultaneously lifts up her hand with a mobile phone in it. There's a sharp click of a light switch.*

SCENE 7

DAISY: I could. Call. I should call her.

She yells sideways to whoever can help.

> I'm sorry, I know I said I wanted to do this without help but I'm thinking maybe now is a good time to reconsider the birth plan. And opt for – *(acute twinge)* – EVERYTHING. LITERALLY EVERYTHING YOU'VE GOT MATE. I PAY MY TAXES, KEEP IT COMING.

Pacing. A massive surge of pain which takes over her whole face and body and is quickly followed by panic. She pulls up a gas and air mouthpiece and sucks deeply.

> Oh my god, I can't do this. I can't have a baby. *(Suck.)* I'll be shit. I can't. *(She yells out suddenly.)* NO. Hullo. Hi there. I've just decided – more discovered really – that I can't do it. Physically. And mentally. Emotionally, and, ultimately, Actually. I mainly Actually can't do it. *(Suck.)* So sorry. You'll have to cancel it. Abort abort. Abandon

the plan Stan. *(Her breath becomes short and she pushes the words out in between.)* Minimise. Close the window. Control Alt Delete. *(Suck.)* Shut down. Cease and desist. Refund. Reverse. Return to sender. Lockdown Lockdown. Permanent hiatus. Out of office. Build a wall. *(Rage.)* WHERE'S MY FUCKING MOTHER. *(Panic.)* Oh god I can't do it without her, I can't do it. I'm going to be a shit mum. Really really bad. *(To her uterus.)* Oh Jesus, is this a joke? How do people do this? OH CHRIST.

DAISY writhes and paces as the pain goes up a few notches. DAISY leans backwards against the bed and lets out a small roar.

The roar is paused, she turns to us:

This is literally the only time you can make this much hell-powered hullabaloo and not look mental. This is your crazy Carte Blanche. Use it. Sod dignity. Sod being the nice girl, Sod manners.

She completes the roar.

UUUURRRRRRGH.

She climbs onto the bed, with difficulty, looking like a dog trying to find a place to shit.

Nurgh. Nurgh god. Oh Jesus. Oh Mary. Oh sweet baby
– *(surge)* –

Beat. Then DAISY properly erupts. It's like The Exorcist.

JESUS GET THIS FUCKING THING OUT OF ME OR I'LL DRAG YOU ALL INTO MY CUNT AND LET THIS DEMON EAT YOU FOR FUCKING LUNCH.

DAISY turns to the audience.

I am so sorry.

Then back to arching her back in pain. She's begging now.

I don't think I can do it. Please get it out of me. I can't do this anymore.

She is composed again; casual.

Why can't birth be more beautiful and delicate? More...

'Girl From Ipanema' sung by Nat King Cole plays and **DAISY** *breaks out her pain and springs from the bed, gracefully like a nymph. She sashays and shimmies around like Audrey Hepburn at a cocktail party as she tells us...*

Growing up, my Mum was the most beautiful woman in the world. We laughed A Lot. We were really funny. We were happy. We were a two-girl party that never ended. Every night she said the same thing as she stood in the bedroom door – good night, sleep tight, don't let the bedbugs bite. And then she'd drift away down the hall to spend the evening doing whatever mysterious things adults do at night.

All I wanted was to look like her. That was my life goal. I used to sniff her Chanel lipsticks and Avon face creams and drape her beads around my neck and let her bangles slip up and down my arm. I was enthralled by it all.

I didn't see a woman dangerously thin and desperately sad. Didn't know she cried after she put me to bed. Good night, sleep tight, don't let the bedbugs bite. Didn't know we were poor now that we didn't live with Dad, who I barely remembered anyway. Didn't know it's hard and lonely raising a kid on your own. Didn't know that the reason we counted pennies out of a big old Gilbys gin bottle for bread and milk was because that's all we had. I just thought we tipped the pennies out and spread them out on the kitchen floor because it was fun. And silvers were a prize hiding in a sea of bronze; you leapt on those. Being sent out on an errand with a tight little palmful of silvers felt like freedom. Cut past the boat yard, duck down and round to the corner shop by the Kursaal. Tin of Go Kat then home without dawdling.

Didn't know Mum was a woman who had run away
from a man she still loved because he was just too damn
hard to be with, that she was struggling to survive every
day. I was too young to see all that. I just saw the beauty.
My Mum was my whole world. A little gem of glamour
in our scruffy seaside town. We lived down Victoria, just
off the front, near the arcades and the bright lights. And
we had the sea. How lucky is that. Who gets to live right
by the sea? Well, the Thames, but close enough. You
can't tell Southenders it's just a river; because they know
it is bigger than that. Living by the water links you up to the
whole world – that stuff is always moving. One minute
it's between your toes in Southend, then hours later that
water could be anywhere. France, the Med, the Atlantic,
you'll never know. You can't track water. And that means
a part of you is out there too. Living by the water makes
you visible, makes you exist. Makes you ancient; timeless.

Mum and I sang on Saturday mornings as we cleaned
the house – the air thick with polish. We both liked it
all to be nice. Clean and shiny. We sang Neil Sedaka
and Carole King and Motown. Big old belters like Lady
Marmalade.

Bit of 'Lady Marmalade' by LaBelle plays.

Mum taught me how to harmonise. I learned to find the
notes a third above or below, and from then on songs
became adventures I could be part of. Belting out a song
at full volume, God that was joy. Me and my mum and
a song. You couldn't buy that; that was our version of
being rich.

'Beautiful' by Carole King plays and **DAISY** *sings along.*

While we cleaned Mum'd tell me about the time she
was in a three-girl band in the 70s called Lady Luck.
Hazel, Jan and Mum. They wore skimpy costumes,
platform boots and marabou fur. Gigged at the Marquee,
Dingwalls, Camden Palace, Stringfellows, drank at
Peppermint Park, and toured round Germany in a

knackered old Bedford van, playing to the troops. One night at a posh do in Park Lane, Tito and Jermaine Jackson – who were footloose, Michael-free and waiting to headline – hopped on stage with them.

Who the hell can say that they played with the Jacksons?

As I got older Mum'd tell me more. How she turned up one day at Hazel's squat in Swiss Cottage to help her audition piano players, to find her naked in an old tin bath in the middle of the lounge. How Hazel leapt across the room, soaking the floor, when she remembered she had a bag of coke hidden in the piano. Well, I thought that was punk rock before I'd even heard of punk.

I'd stare up at the big sepia photograph of Mum on the wall and wonder if I'd ever be anything like her.

We see a picture of **DAISY***'s mum. This also draws* **TAG** *back on stage. There's a loud revving of an engine.*

SCENE 8

TAG: *YOUR MATES ARE OUTSIDE*

What?

I SAID YOUR MATES ARE OUTSIDE!!!!

Ever since a horrendous for all involved entry of the room mid masturbation, my mum keeps a strict outside the door policy to message giving. I nip into my old man's cupboard in the toilet and slap a bit of his Cool Water on my chops. Ben Sherman collar pulled up tight. China white jeans cling to my legs. Toe tappers on. Nicely shined. And we're off down the stairs.

Don't you be home too late. You've got a big day tomorrow.

Mum's already trying to fuss but an unlikely and unprompted kiss of her cheek sends her scurrying back to the sofa and Pat and Frank Butcher's latest Abbey

Domestic. Found her in tears in the kitchen the other day watching Emmerdale. She's not taking it well. Proud, but still… You know. Nests. Empty ones.

EMMERDALE! We are not an Emmerdale household!

Can hear my old man saying it. Like it's some kind of disease being a Northerner. Fuck knows what he is going to do when he has to come and visit. But tonight's not about that. Tonight we can all just crack on and pretend that everything will stay the same. Forever and ever, Amen.

He slips his hand in my back pocket as I'm heading out the door. Winks at me. And it's a funny thing the old man wink. It operates completely without making him look like a paedo. So in a way, is a rare and wonderful sight.

Have one on me, boy.

I try and tell him that it's alright. That I'm sorted. That him and mum have done enough already. But it's just back slaps and non paedo winks as he pushes me out the door. And I'm a score up on the night already.

Winner winner, chicken dinner.

The car is sat there in the road waiting for me. The green fluorescent tubes under the chassis lighting up my shitty caul de sac like it's Christmas Day.

You gonna get in or just stand there like a lemon?

Gal. My best mate. My lie down in front of traffic for me mate. Nice lad. Tall. Never had a scrap. Never had a bird. Potentially likes blokes. But Thurrock, Essex, is not a place to explore the frontiers of your sexuality at this precise moment. And what he lacks in violence and chat up lines he makes up in hard wear…

A canary yellow Vauxhall Nova GTI. Machine gun exhaust. Induction kit. Eighteen inch split rim alloy wheels. Braided brake lines. Forged pistons. Carbon and rear splitter. Spoiler the size of the Eiffel tower. Stereo system that could play the Pyramid stage at Glastonbury. And a Turbo under the bonnet that would make a Porsche 911 blush.

Come on mate, we're late as it is. Gonna be rammo up there already.

Bombhead. The Laurel to Gal's Hardy. You'd think with a name like Bombhead, Bomb might be a hard as nails bastard. Popular.

He's not.

He's called Bombhead coz when he was twelve his face exploded in acne. It's virtually gone now. But the name stuck.

Let me in then, you dick.

This is all part of a careful routine we've been performing to the residents of Colville Close every Thursday, Friday, Saturday and occasionally Sunday night since Gal got his car. Since we got our passports.

Bombhead gets out. As soon as he has I casually call 'Shotgun'.

You can't call shotgun when I've already been sitting in the seat.

His reserve is going to last exactly a minute. I know this. He knows this. Even the little old lady at number twenty-six stood by the window cursing at us for playing music this loudly knows.

Shotgun rules mate.

This is bollocks.

You can't mess with the ten commandments. And you definitely can't mess with shotgun rules.

One of you dickheads get in the fucking back. We're late.

I don't move a muscle. Just keep staring at Bomb's stupid mug.

This. Is. Bollocks.

He gets in the back. Careful not to sit in the seat that we never sit in. The one seat that no one can call shotgun on. Eternally reserved.

We don't talk about that. It's one of the many things we don't talk about. Me and my mates. My best mates. My –

The door slams and finally the night can begin. Gal floors the motor and we wheel spin out of the road like we're making a jail break. Forty minutes till we hit the front. Forty minutes till we are with our people again. The boy and girl racers. The day trippers who just want to take a glimpse. The pissheads looking for a ruck. The birds. The blokes. The –

I suppose it's only right you having the front seat. This being your last night out on The Cruise.

There's a silence. An awkwardness. We had managed to avoid this conversation.

It's not going to be my last cruise.

I say it. But the words are hollow. Empty. And they know. My best mates. My lie down in front of traffic for me mates.

Fuck going back to school. Especially up north. You've lost the plot mate.

Gal won't use the word university. It's a hand grenade. He could have gone. Ten A stars in his exams. His mum and dad ain't like mine though. First week after school had finished he was down the garage with his old man. Grease on his hands.

And I wonder sometimes if Gal really does like cars. Or if he just accepted his fate. Bowed down to it. An easy life.

Wonder what the birds will be like up there? Manchester.

Bombhead has a moment of true wonder where he thinks that me moving to another city might lead to him losing his V plates.

They're northern mate, they ain't blind.

Me and Gal crack up laughing. And Bombhead slumps back in his seat. But secretly we're all a bit happy at the change in conversation. At the return to bullshit lad banter. That we can move on. That we can ignore the gigantic fucking elephant that's sat in the car with us. This new elephant. To add to the others. On this night.

This last night.

Samba music creeps in ('A Voz Do Morro' by Ze Keti).

Seventy miles per hour...

Seventy-five...

Eighty...

Eighty-five...

Ninety...

Ninety-five...

And we blur into the night like a star behind a set of clouds.

Something changes.

SCENE 9

The air is hotter, thicker. It is the air you breathe abroad, full of expectations. **FIZA**
*listens to the music and clumsily tries to dance to it. Realising Samba is insanely difficult
she gives up.*

FIZA: I'm in Salvador de Bahia, Brazil, it's 2006. I feel like I've escaped! Here I belong to the night sky. To the stars, and the sea. Who said identity has to be tied to geography?

As I watch the reflection of the lights dance on the water in the marina a man exclaims, "I've heard all about you Romford girls." In my broken Brazilian Portuguese I ask him, "what the actual fuck?" He tells me he doesn't understand how a person like me can be English.

Does he mean because I'm brown? I try to explain the British Raj, partition and multiculturalism in my **still** very broken Portuguese, but it doesn't translate.

"No," he says. "Because you have assimilated into the land of the oppressor. I would have expected better from you." OOF.

An invisible punch to the gut. It hurts. The music fades.

That is the last time I tell people I'm from Romford for a while.

All I remember of this place, this place I grew up in, is being a misfit. This place that isn't here nor there, that's caught in between two worlds, borders the city, borders the county and creates borders within me. Borders that separate the things that make me fit, and those that make me stand out like a sore thumb. Being here again triggers me. I feel out of place, out of sorts. I am too loud for this place.

There are several locations within ten minutes walk from my parents house, that offer a tantalising glimpse of London.

1. Brentwood Road. Not long after Frances Bardsley but before the shell garage on your right and the Evangelical church on your left, as you descend into Romford. There it is! Canary Wharf! Got to be quick though, by the time you hit the Jehovah's Witness Hall it's disappeared.

2. Hillcrest Road. As you exit Hylands Park onto Hylands Way and look to your right, down Hillcrest Road, at the right time of day, in the right conditions, it peeks out from the skyline, smiling at me. Teasing.

It feels like I spent my childhood living in its shadow, dreaming of the time I'd be able to call it home. Dreaming of belonging.

I lived in London for five years, with him; he ruined it for me. We met at an upmarket Romford establishment.

The sound of a crowded restaurant/auditorium.

I was the waitress and he was the barman. It went under a little while after we had both stopped working there, which I suppose is a relief now, although at the time it felt devastating, like we'd lost our origin story.

I have to pass that place every time I go to Romford station. And even though it's another completely different establishment, the shadow of its past, of my failure, will sit with me on the train all the way into Liverpool Street.

ALEXA *chimes a reminder notification.*

ALEXA: I'm reminding you to RSVP to the reunion.

SCENE 10

Four days later. The Kursaal. We hear a grandfather clock ticking. **JOANNA** *is outside Mr Bacon's office.*

JOANNA: I wouldn't call myself stupid because I know I'm not. And despite being able to only read and write a bit, it's important to remember that 'Writing and reading does not a clever person make'; *(Tapping her head.)* You've got to have it up here too. I know quite a few white folk, who are well educated, even went to university, but thick as anything. And so, this is why, me; a clever woman, being here, at this very moment, makes for no sense whatsoever, because everything, and believe me when I say everything – every skin flake, every hair, every breath, is telling me to get up and walk out that door, and yet here/

(Speaking to his secretary.) / Excuse me Mam, could you please pass my thanks onto Mr Bacon, it's just that I no longer…and there he is, standing in the doorway of his office.

Joanna Barlow?

Oh, fudge! – Yes, I am Joanna Barlow. Actually, I'm Joanna Mbalow but I thought if I told you that, you wouldn't see me.

I don't like liars. And you, Madam, (Correcting himself) Woman – are a liar. And a Negro liar at that. See yourself out.

(Speaking quickly.) I believe pageants are God's way of allowing us to admire his creations on a stage. In fact, call it blasphemy, but I'd even go as far as to say they perhaps enable us to stop, and admire God himself, since he did indeed create us, in his own image.

I recognise you. You're that crazy Negro who put her hand up in church on Sunday. Gave us all a good laugh that did. I've never met a funny Negro before.

I explain that many of us speak English too.

And yours I must say, is very good.

Mr Bacon – I'd like to tell you why I came. I came here, Mr Bacon, sir, to ask you favour; to beg you in fact for an act of good will –

Time is money Miss, and one thing this place is doing well at is losing money.

(*Firmly.*) Mr Bacon – you are going to enter me into your beauty pageant.

He's stood. Staring. Then asks if this is some kind Negro joke.

I'm extremely serious Mr Bacon. It's time for a change. Never has a woman of my colour entered a pageant in this country. I'm not expecting to win – but I do feel the time has come for us –

Are you mad?

Clearly he doesn't want people to think that he's some sort of Negro sympathiser. I try to assure him that they won't – well, not all of them anyway.

And then he did something I've never seen a fully grown man do (*Placing her hands over her ears and singing lots of 'La la la's'*) What is he doing? What are you doing Mr Bacon? Stop it! Stop it! (*She mimes struggling to take his hands off his ears – there's a tussle. Eventually* **JOANNA** *wins.*)

Look, I've never hit a woman before, but there's a first time for everything. So why don't you toodle off Princess and fight your cause elsewhere?!

(**JOANNA** *freezes on the spot.*) Mr Bacon, could you please say that again.

What? I've never hit a woman…

No not that!

So why don't you toodle off Princess and –

Mr Bacon, as I said, you will enter me into your beauty pageant but not as myself. Instead, you'll enter me into this town's biggest beauty contest under the pretence of being … an African Princess.

Get out! I mean it! Get out!

You said you need the money. I assume you're looking for profit **and** publicity – Yes? Think, Mr Bacon – You could be known forever as the man responsible for the first ever *(Thinking of a term.)* Chocolate hued woman to win a pageant in the whole of Great Britain. Think.

He asks me what I'd call her, this African Princess.

(Thinking.) Princess…Din…no…bo…lu…of…Senegal?? *(Standing upright.)* I, am Princess Dinubolu of Senegal.

He then asks me if I know anything about African Royalty. I explain that whilst my knowledge is pretty thin, I doubt anybody else round here knows more than we do, so let's play up to the stereotype and just give the people what they want.

I'm sorry, but it's a no. I've worked hard to get to where I am today – I'm a well-respected member of this community. If this went wrong – and it would – my wife would never forgive me – we'd have to leave the area – (He gasps) move to the countryside – we'd 'go for walks' – I'm not ready for that – I'm only forty – I don't want people to think I have anything to do with your kind.

Not even one of my kind who is rich, educated, beautiful, confident, and so high up the social ladder you and I could only dream of it?

He stands there for a second, weighing up the odds.

Believe me when I say I've a lot to lose as well. If this did go wrong, it would have implications for not only myself, but my sister Mary who I love more than anyone else in the entire world – she's all I've got. I would lose my job, and it's not as if I can just find another. And where would I live? How would I hide? I can't just blend into the background – look at me. *(Reassuringly.)* I'm not planning on telling anyone, are you?

SCENE 11

TAG: Behind my house are the train tracks that go from
Southend to London. The fast train. Once or twice a
year though they send a maintenance train up them.
About two in the morning.

When I was a kid I used to wake up and all the lights
from it would just blast through my curtains and
illuminate my room. Like aliens were landing. Right
there. At the end of my bed.

Like it was the end of the world.

I never really slept that well as a kid. When you know
that once or twice a year an alien might shine a light
through your window it kind of puts a stop to that. I used
to try and tell my mum and dad, but they wouldn't listen.
They didn't understand. The only person who ever did
was my mate Luke.

A moment.

Luke was the fourth musketeer.
The empty seat in Gal's car.
My best mate.
My lie down in front of traffic for me mate.
He wasn't like Gal and Bombhead.
He talked.
He had feelings.
He knew.
He knew about this town.
And some time in year ten he just stopped smiling.
It wasn't a gradual thing.
Something that passes you by.
He just stopped one day.
Might have been a lunchbreak
Or after school on the way home.
Or during Science with Mr Cobb.
But it happened.

And then some nights he'd say he couldn't be bothered
to come out up the park.
He couldn't be bothered to get pissed.
He couldn't be bothered to try and talk to girls

To breathe.

He took a walk up those tracks.
The ones that lead to London.
The ones that the aliens would come down.
He took a walk one night
And he…

He didn't come back.

And I sometimes think about how cold it must have been.
And I wonder what he was thinking.
Or if he was thinking…

I wonder if he thought of me.

The sound of a train starts to build.

And that last conversation that we had.
Those words.
I wonder if they meant as much to him as they do to me.

Get out mate. Get out while you can.

SCENE 12

July 1908. Morning of the Pageant. We see **JOANNA** *sitting in a third class train carriage. She is wearing an expensive looking, bright red, Western style dress. She has a newspaper resting on her lap. The sound of a steam train speeding along the tracks.*

JOANNA: The Estuary. I love it. When I was little, Mary and I, we'd
stand holding hands looking out to sea. I would tell Mary
that I could see the sea waving at me, and she in turn would
always respond with, *"Joanna – That's scientifically impossible
because the sea doesn't have hands" (Beat.)* She had a point.
Mary's always been right – she's the Mum I never had.
Dad did an alright job, but it's only now I'm older, that I

realise Mary sacrificed a lot of her own life for mine. She must have bore the brunt of a lot of hatred when we were growing up.

Tilbury.

Until today, I'd never been to London before – aren't there a lot of people? *So* many people. Nowhere needs to be that big. And the air – it's so dense – you can't breathe. Fantastic buildings though. And you should have seen some of the clothes, some of them rich folk wore colours I'd never seen before.

(Remembering she is in an elegant red dress.) I'm not convinced that red is really me. Well, not *me* of course – Princess Dinubolu. *(Referring to her dress.)* I got given this by Mr Bacon this morning just before I got taken in a coach to Fenchurch Street. Bless 'im, he handed it over with much pride, and told me that he'd actually bought it for his wife, just before they married a few years ago, but in the three years since, apparently both he and her have put on quite a bit of weight. *(Thinking)* It doesn't really fit me either; size wise 'yes', but it feels like I'm wearing someone else's skin – but it's too late to turn back now, *(Beat.)* init?

(Beginning to panic.) I did say, I know <u>nothing</u> of African royalty. As it happens, after my initial meeting with Mr Bacon, my walk home took me via the statue of Queen Victoria. As I looked up, I thought, what is it, apart from the crown, that makes you *Queen* Victoria and not just *Victoria*? **(JOANNA** *adjusts herself as she speaks.)* She sits upright – shoulders back, she smiles – but not too much, her eyes are direct – she knows what she wants, her finger points toward the sea with absolute conviction. Maybe we'd all sit like that if we owned half the world.

Leigh-on-Sea!

I lied. I told Mr Bacon that I wouldn't tell a soul. I'm pretty sure I would have told Mary at some point, but before I even had a chance to, she'd already found out. She'd discovered it, as she was serving tea. Her Master was reading aloud an article from one of the National Papers, and turned it round to reveal the artist's impression. Mary knew straight away, that underneath all the zebra skin, feathers, and beaded jewellery was her one and only sister.

It started with *(Pointing to herself.)* 'A source' contacting the local papers, to tell them that a Senegalese Princess had applied to enter Southend's Summer Beauty Pageant, and unlike Warwick, Bristol, Brighton, Salisbury, and Great Yarmouth for example, who all have colour-bars, *technically* Southend doesn't, well not on paper, so therefore Princess Dinubolu would be heading to Essex as she was as free to enter the contest as her non-negro counterparts.

Mary screamed at me. She's never spoken to me like that. I tried to tell her, I'm doing this *for* her. For Adele. And yes, a little bit for myself.

(Looking out the window.) Look at it. Just look at it. The water. God it's beautiful, init? *(Pause.)* Makes you think. *(She laughs.)* 'Senegal' – never been, but you know why I like the sound of it? Listen. *(Saying it slowly.)* Sen-e-gal. *(Pause.)* Sounds a bit like, 'seagull'. *(The sound of seagulls.)*

I remember one day when I was small, my best friend Henry and I playing down on beach just by the pier – we were collecting shells for a game of jacks, when Henry let out this almighty scream…

We hear the sound of a scream transforming into a train whistle.

SCENE 13

Neon light. Noise. Car engines. Life.

TAG:

BOOOOOOOOOOOOOOOOOOOOOOOOOOOOOOOOOM

The shitty estuary air wafts in the open car window that I'm using to flick fag ash out of. Gal has already gone through the standard smoking policy of the car.

If you burn something I will kill you quicker than cancer.

We take the cut through via Old Leigh so we can build up a bit of speed for our entrance to The Cruise. On the side of the road the sea glistens in the moonlight.

This is our place.

Our home.

Gal has got the car absolutely flying now and is trying to break into three digits before we hit the speed camera near the casino.

Eighty-five

Ninety

Ninety –

Who the fuck is this prick?

Two headlights are approaching us from behind at speed. And when I say speed, we are doing at least ninety-five by now. And they are catching us like we're an old lady in a Fiat Panda out doing her weekly shop.

Mate, get out of the lane!

It's my lane

Have you seen what car it is?

There's only one car on the whole strip that can make Gal look slow. One set of wheels that can show him up like this.

It's Her.

A dump valve cracks through the air. The White RS Cosworth moves within inches of the back of us. And Gal knows there's nothing he can do. He swerves into the centre of the road allowing her to pass. Her tinted window ever so slightly open. Her pink acrylic fingernails wrapped round the pure white Embassy menthol cigarette. Then she's gone.

Gal is fuming.

I would have had her if she didn't just appear from nowhere like that.

And lying.

Yeah mate.

Bombhead senses the wound to his ego and starts to tend to it like the fat spotty Essex equivalent of Florence Nightingale.

You wanna say something rather than just stare out the window like some kind of fucking gimp?

My silence is taken as an act of betrayal. I remedy this immediately. The night is balanced on very fine set of scales as it is.

Yeah course you could have had her mate.

But he couldn't. No one could. No one ever has. She stands undefeated on the A127.

Shall we nip in an offie? I'm already out of vodka.

Bombhead knows the drill. Distraction. The only way to get Gal out of a night wrecking mood. And tonight can't be wrecked.

In the silent moments I can feel that knot that I've been carrying round in my stomach for the last few months continue to grow. A cancer to hope. To adventure. To something new. It's a local disease.

Get out mate. Get out while you can.

But now I am getting out. Now everything feels a bit too real. A bit too…

Now.

What am I going to do in Manchester?

I'm a Blur man. Fuck Oasis.

University? Me? Yeah, I did alright in my school. But basically all that was required there was being able to write actual words rather than draw cartoon dicks on your books.

They're going to find me out.

I know it.

Even from the few people I met when we went up there for an interview. My old man driving me round the universities. Him telling me about how great it's going to be. How him and my mum would have loved to have these opportunities. How different it all is now.

Life.

But maybe I don't want it to be. Maybe I want what he has. Maybe I want to stay there in that shithole town that I grew up in. Maybe I don't want to learn anything else. Maybe I've learnt enough already.

Get out mate. Get out while you can.

Dead arms rain down on me.

What do you want to fucking drink you bellend!

Six stella and a half bottle of voddy.

I slap my old man's score into Bombhead's hand and he jumps out of the motor and makes a mad dash for the offie. And that just leaves me and Gal in the car. Me, Gal and the empty seat where Luke should be sitting.

How's things going at your dad's garage?

Yeah, good, yeah.

You definitely knocking the idea of going to college on the head?

What do I want to go to college for?

You said –

Earning money now ain't I. That's why we're sat here in a proper motor rather than your shitty Metro City.

My car is always a source of great amusement to Gal. My old man bought it for me for my birthday. I just shrug and laugh.

Call me when you breakdown on your way to Manchester.

And with that the keys are turned over. The engine dies. And he's out the door. I wonder if Gal feels that I've betrayed him. Leaving. Another one of us.

When Luke…

When he…

It hit Gal hard.

Do you want to tap a fag?

He's not a smoker. Not like me and Bomb. But occasionally when there's a note of tension in the air, like there is tonight, you can lure him into one.

I will be back you know.

He smokes.

Probably get kicked out when they realise I'm just a dumb Essex p−

You ain't dumb. Don't say that kind of shit. Enough people hear how we talk and assume it. Don't need to give them an excuse to think it.

Sorry.

And don't say sorry. I'm proud of you. We all are…

Luke would be too.

There is a silence. It's happening. I'm leaving. I know it. Gal knows it. My mum and dad know it. And that's why we can talk like this. That's why Gal can say that word and he can mean it. Proud.

And I want to hold him. I want to say that I'm proud of him too. That I love the bones of the boy. I always have.

But I can't.

Coz that's not what people do round here.

But it doesn't matter.

Cor, you nick them lights off your mum's Christmas tree?

I turn and see a dude wearing a cowboy hat about five yards away from Gal. Behind him a Black Honda Civic.

See you get done by that slag in the White Cosworth earlier an all. Might as well give me the keys and I'll take that heap of shit down the scrapper for you.

You wanna watch your mouth.

Or what?

Or I'll shut it.

The Cowboy takes the cigarette out of his mouth and flicks it straight at Gal. It misses and bounces off Gal's car leaving a small smudge of ash against the bodywork. And I take this as my cue to get in-between them before it's handbags and glad rags time.

Woah woah woah woah lads. What's going on?

Did you see what that prick just did?

Gal's shouting over my arms as I try and hold him back. There's a feeling you get when you're holding someone back. You know whether they want you to, or whether they want to fight. But at this precise moment I couldn't tell you which.

Prick? You think a dickhead in his mum's car can call me a prick?

The Cowboy wants it. That much is clear…

You think you're fast?

I know I'm fast.

Prove it.

A127. You know the spot. Midnight.

Done.

Call yourself a paramedic to come and collect you after.

Then he's gone. Disappeared back into his car. The wheel spin and smell of burning rubber all that's left when Bombhead bounces back across the street

Did you see that motor? Speed on toast.

Just get in the car, Bomb.

What did I say?

Something changes.

SCENE 14

DAISY: For years I never put two and two together that the end of my mum's music career came just as she got pregnant with me. That was a shock to realise. Not that she ever said it. I just…caught up I guess. Woman to woman, level somehow, like 'ohhh… right'.

Mum, who did all those fun things, who looked like a film star, who let her voice ring out like a bell, who could command a crowd of braying soldiers, who got accompanied by a couple of excited Jacksons, who could keep taking a song higher and higher. Mum, who grew up in poverty, brothers running round barefoot and selling church roof tiles, Mum who lost her hair with nerves aged two, alopecia, curly grew back straight, who got taken into foster care, survived two loveless households, who visited her mum on weekends – her poor not-quite-dead mum, semi-paralysed in a chair, abused by men who'd been broken by war and work – only words she ever heard her mum mumble were "she's mine" – imagine being locked in your body and watching your baby go. Mum, who escaped Essex, who fled to London, who lived, who found music, who found love, who survived love, who escaped back to Essex, who did all that, is now just here, now, with you, and is just

Your mum.

All you see is your mum.

She never stops being any of that.

But inside her is all that stuff she was before – she never stops being that. As she's grating cheese on your beans on toast or brushing your hair or driving you everywhere, she never stops being any of that. She just stores it all under being your mum. Like a bag of old stuff she might pull out and go through when you've gone to bed.

This was me, and this was me. And oh my sweet
hotpants, this was me. God. I was – *so fantastic*.

A burst of bright stage lights, the sound of floodlights being switched on.

SCENE 15

The Kursaal. **JOANNA** *is standing with her head turned to the left/right.* **JOANNA** *is
last in line to find out how well (or badly) she's done. We hear a loud cheer.*

JOANNA: I'm not expecting to win. I just know. We all know. I
can't. But that's not to say I haven't won the battle, and
achieved all that I set out to and more. Because here I
am; Me – Joanna Elizabeth Mbalow standing in front of
3000 people making history, and let's remember, history
does not forget moments like this. Granted, only time
will tell whether what I have achieved today is incredible
or incredibly stupid, but regardless, today is a *moment* in
Essex History – it happened, I made it happen, *(Correcting
herself)* Princess Dinubolu made it happen.

The sound of applause. **JOANNA** *is pacing – she's received some bad news.*

I will be sad to say goodbye to Princess Dinubolu. Because
of her, I have for the first time in my life been *seen* and
when the people looked, they liked what they saw – they
didn't cross the road, scuttle past, or gaze at me in a way
that made me feel more animal than human.

Reacting to another polite round of applause.

This is the end of Round One. It involved myself and
the other contestants having to parade across the stage
– and now, with us all having done it, we are in the
process of finding out who's going through to Round
Two. Interestingly enough, here at The Kursaal, it is
not a panel of judges who decide the winners but the
audience by way of round of applause. There are several
categories we can enter ourselves in for; I decided upon
'Best Hair', 'Best Brunette' and just for hundreds and

thousands, 'Best Blonde'. *(Remembering.)* Oh! And of course, best 'Overall'. *(Noticing she's next.)* One sec.

The applause continues.

SCENE 16

DAISY *becomes her mum. Centre-stage, getting ready for a show. She zips up some killer platform boots. She's fabulous. This is how a night in her mum's old life might have gone. 1978. She pulls a mic stand to the front. She clicks and the lights change. She clicks and conjures the sound of a jack being plugged in, PA hum, sound check, a bass guitar noodling about, the roll of sticks on a snare, a muted thrash of a hammond organ.* **DAISY** *prowls, warming up her legs and voice, running her tongue around her mouth, squatting, stretching her arms, getting show ready. Says 1-2 into the mic. Cups her hand over her eyes and scans the audience.*

DAISY: Hey Frank. Can you get me a whisky? You're a darling. *(She laughs.)* Yeah, I'd marry you. If I didn't think you'd make a terrible husband and I'd be a very bored and bad housewife. Let's just keep things as they are shall we. *(Beat. Laughs.)*

She necks a whisky. The lights change. She grasps the mic stand and strikes a show pose.

Good evening ladies and gents, how are we all tonight? Lady Luck is in the house and she is hot to trot. We're going to sing a few songs that we just know you already love.

The sound of an audience. Cheering. Clapping. **DAISY** *hits her heel on the floor, stirring them up. The opening bars of 'Lady Marmalade'.* **JOANNA** *takes a deep breath and steps forward. The crowd erupts.* **JOANNA** *stands there in complete shock.*

JOANNA: I've only gone and fudging done it! Goodbye Mabel! Tut tar Irene! Make way for the African Queen! *(Becoming pompous.)* After Round One comes Round Two – a chance for *us* contestants to address the public, and tell them why they should vote for us to be their *Miss Southend 1908. Obviously* I wasn't expecting to get this far, but I don't need to say much – the people **love** me!

The music halts. **DAISY** *stares up at the blinding lights. She breathes deep, tired from her show, but full of glory. As she stares up at the stage lights, her smile drops, fades, her face changes until what's left – is fear.*

DAISY:　　　　And you realise, that what happened to your mum is about to happen to you. You are about to give up so much. You are about to stop – being seen.

The lights dim. It's quiet. **DAISY** *clears away the mic stand; the gig's over. But something is plaguing her…*

DAISY:　　　　She wanted more for me. Mum. She wanted me to have more than she had. That's natural. But I just felt stifled.

We had a stupid, stupid row – putting up the cot. Squished together on our hands and knees in the box room like two old cows at milking time. Mum just suddenly sat back, threw down the screws. Said "A man'd just know how to do this, automatically" and I thought 'Fuck the hell no mother. No.' and I just snapped. Told her it was all her fault. Told her I was shit and broken because she couldn't manage doing anything normal. That because I didn't stand a chance how could my baby stand a chance. Generations of lost chances. I threw all that at her. *(She nods.)* Yeah. *(Beat.)* We haven't spoken since.

I think some of the anger was because in that one stupid sentence about a man knowing how to do everything – she had reduced every struggle she'd overcome, all on her own. Because if she doesn't see what a fucking warrior she was, if what she did is *normal*, how will I ever come close?

I was angry *for* her, not *at* her. *(Pause.)* I should've told her that.

DAISY *sits on the edge of the bed, pulls her legs up and lets them fall open. She unzips the boots and lets them fall to the floor.*

Back to the pain. She lands back on the bed.

ALEXA: I'm reminding you to RSVP to the reunion.

FIZA: One member of the class of 2001 is currently performing on Broadway, one works at CERN and another is like in government or something. Then there's the one who used to be famous, but no one listens to his band anymore. Those who left school at sixteen and went to work in the city now own half of Emerson Park. Facebook tells me they have husbands, wives, babies, doctorates, live in far-off places – So you see why someone might feel insecure about being around these people after twenty years?

Not someone…me. The me who was brought up on the immigrant dream. The work hard and you'll get everything you deserve mentality. It'll just plop into your lap. And if it doesn't, it means you didn't try hard enough. Except it doesn't work like that, does it? Cause sometimes you work hard, so very hard and it still falls apart. Sometimes you work so hard *you* fall apart.

I work for a children's charity. It's not big, or exciting, or shiny. It won't get me a house, but it is very rewarding. I wish that were enough.

He was a high-flier. Single minded and stubborn. Never took his eye off the ball, everything in pursuit of the end goal – the PhD, the big career, the life I guess he'd never dared to dream for himself. Single parent working class, first in his family to go to uni despite not finishing school. As soon as he hit the jackpot he was out of here. Upped and moved North. I wonder if he's unpacking right now too?

The smaller box glows in response.

All the sentimental things you accumulate when you're building a life together. I wonder will he keep them… or if they never even made the cut, and are sitting in a landfill in Rainham. Ironically closer to me than I feel comfortable with.

Recognising that this is not a question that will end well the box comes to life. 'Born Slippy' by Underworld plays. **FIZA** *is dubious, she never really liked this song. She approaches cautiously and takes a look in. A woosh to signify that we're in a place that's in the past. A Bacardi Breezer appears and* **FIZA** *reads the ingredients list, but then realises she's probably having a breakdown so what do chemicals matter anyway? As she drinks, the memory comes to life.*

1996, and Underworld has put Romford on the map. Suddenly everyone has forgotten about the episode of Boozed Up Britain featuring Romford High Street. A few of us celebrate with alcopops under the big roundabout by the marketplace and later go to the ice-rink.

Cheers!

Romford ice rink. Remember that place? Before Saphire & Ice. Before the Liberty Centre, before we discovered Shoreditch, before we could hit the big boy clubs. This is what teenagers do. This is normal. Is this the moment I am *finally* normal?

I remember how short-lived the celebration is. We've barely got started before I get into a fight with a girl from the year below me. Someone told me she called me a paki. I don't know if I heard it with my own ears. The more I exclaim "I'm not drunk".

(To the audience.) I'm not drunk!

The more they tell me I am. I am drunk. Drunk on the conflicting feelings coursing through my veins.

The song hits its peak, arms in the air.

I lose myself in the moment. Skate circles. I spin, or at least try to.

She spins until she can spin no longer.

I wonder what she's doing now. The racist girl from the year below. Bet she's living her best life in the current climate. Do you know that in the last three years I have blocked and unfriended no less than seven people I went to school with. Why? For upholding views that violate the human rights of others. Views that invalidate me and my brown skin. I do enough of that myself thank you very much. Don't really need you to pile it on too. My problem isn't that I don't know how to assimilate, it's that no one would let me.

If there's any booze left, she drinks it now. She's woozy.

My husband was a misfit too. First time I met him one half of his hair was a completely different colour to the other. He looked…stupid.

She takes a moment to remember him. From somewhere the opening of 'This Modern Love' by Bloc Party plays. We can barely hear it, but it calls to **FIZA**. *She listens, trying to work out exactly where it's coming from (the smaller box). By the time the lyrics have kicked in, it's faded.*

But he came later.

She wants to hold onto that memory, restart the song, but it won't. A light starts to shine out of the large box, it catches **FIZA***'s eye. She peers in. Emotion almost overwhelms her. She takes out a fake candle and stands silently, sombre.*

The year after Kurt Cobain died a girl in my year held a…memorial? I don't know what else to call it. We gathered at her house, hunchbacks in negligees weighed down by the unbearable angst of being a misunderstood teen. We felt the loss of Kurt would be too heavy to bear, but by sharing stories, our collective pain soon transformed into a healing balm.

I walked home from the ceremony feeling a fullness that you can't achieve from food. The first time I recognise feeling that way.

As I strutted down the road I saw three guys, kids really. I know them. I've seen them before. They've chased me out of HMV before shouting, grunger bitch! Because that's the worst of my many identities? Today they see me in full riot girl mode and they chase me until I have a stitch and am forced to stop. They laugh at me and spit. I stand in Harrow Lodge Park with saliva in my hair relieved that at least it's got nothing to do with my ethnicity.

Someone, somewhere is playing 'The Last Post' on a trumpet.

In the morning we woke up to find the p-word scrawled on my dad's car.

She begins to climb under her bed. 'Soft Shock' by Yeah Yeah Yeah plays.

I've been sleeping on the floor since I got here. There's an ex-husband shaped imprint on one third of the mattress. Damn memory-foam. I take responsibility for overspooning the boundary. He liked to curl into a sort of c shape right at the end of the bed. Almost hanging out…out of the bed, out of the relationship.

Did I not try hard enough? Was my voice not soft enough? Did I not take my mother-in-law's racism lightly enough? Did I not sweep things under the carpet enough? Should I have apologised more?

Is it really a successful marriage if you realise you're being neglected and continue to lie down for more?

She pulls her covers with her under the bed.

I presume you are capable of showing yourselves out.

SCENE 18

TAG: Fiesta XR2. Saxo VTR. Peugeot GTI. Clio GT. Suped up Golf. Nissan Skyline. And the obligatory blue and gold drug dealer Subaru Impreza. This is what I can see out of the window. The cars pass us as they complete their circle of the esplanade. The circuit. The cruise. The lads and lasses driving them, they'll be here next week. So will Gal. And Bombhead. But me? Who knows.

I'm halfway down the bottle of Kiwi Mad Dog that Bombhead bought me.

I decide what you're drinking on your last night.

Gal has barely said a word since the altercation with the Cowboy. Bomb has been quizzing him since he got back about the race, wrecking his head about it.

The booze is starting to hit me hard. I can feel the beads of sweat on my forehead starting to form. I need some air. In another life I would be tucked up in bed. Suitcase packed next to me. Waiting for tomorrow to come. Waiting for my new life to begin. But It's Friday night. It's the cruise.

Can you open the window a bit mate?

Gal's still deep in his chat with Bombhead about how he is going to show the Cowboy exactly who has the fastest car.

Gal, mate, can you –

What's your problem?

I just need –

What? What do you need?

There is no answer to this question that will make him happy.

Pretty quiet when the Cowboy was giving me shit wasn't you? Proper had my back mate.

Gal…

Might as well have just stayed at home if you didn't want to come.

I did want to come.

*Sat there like a fucking mime all night. Busy imagining all your
new posh mates your gonna make at school eh?*

Mate I just –

Why don't you just fuck off mate.

And maybe it's something to do with the sickness that is
coming for me, maybe it's the fact twenty minutes ago
he was telling me he was proud of me, or maybe it's
the illuminous green Kiwi flavoured Mad Dog washing
round in my body that makes me boot the back of his
seat.

My fucking car!

You fucking child.

I ain't the one going back to school.

And even though I've spent the last few days thinking
very much about doing the same. The words come out
of my mouth. Like a blade.

Nah, you bottled it.

And it strikes deep into his flesh.

Get out.

Gladly.

Lads…

Bombhead is pleading. But I'm already halfway out of
the car and onto the street. Adrenaline coursing through
my veins.

This is our last n –

I'm storming down the road. I'm striding out. Fuck Gal.
Fuck both of them. I'm gone tomorrow. I'm sick of
this bullshit. I'm sick of sitting up here never talking to
birds. I'm sick of a McDonald's on the way home being

the highlight of every Friday night out. I'm almost at the Kursaal. I can almost make out the bright lights of the arcades. The route back to the train station so I can get out of this shitty county once and for all. This shitty county full of these shitty people that I'm sick of. I'm sick to death of. I'm sick…

No. I'm actually sick. I'm going to puke. I jog carefully past a hen party making sure to keep my lips firmly shut. There are ten metres to the alleyway.

Five

Four

Three

Two

Simultaneously

DAISY: And just like that everything kicks in together and – the pain breaks and you're too numb to panic because it's all happening so fast.

Throughout this **DAISY** *slowly arches her back, spreads her legs, and pulls out an endless length of white sheet. Perhaps it starts off red and ends white, then drops to the floor. There's applause and* **JOANNA** *is standing there pacing – she's received some bad news.* **FIZA** *pokes out her head from under the bed and retreats.*

TAG: I wake up and there's a white light at the end of a dark space. I don't believe in God and I'm not sure anyone has ever died before from necking a bottle of MD 20/20 so this is all slightly confusing. Then the stench of my puke wafting up at my nose snaps me back to reality. I'm alive. I suck in the cold night air. And as my senses kick back in I realise that although this might not be heaven, I am in the presence of a God. Or to be more precise a Goddess.

I look up and there she is. Walking down the alley to me. Full white Kappa tracksuit. Pink acrylic nails. Sunglasses even though it's pitch black. The girl in the White Cosworth. Her. And she's talking to me.

I try to stand up but gravity hits me like an apple on the head. I rock back against the wall of the alley. She puts a hand on my arm. Steadies me.

My hand touches hers. An electric shock. Kinetic energy. Lightening.

She sits down next to me. Passes me some water. A stick of Wrigley's spearmint chewing gum.

And I don't know what happens. Because I have grown up knowing this is the one thing you don't do round here. The one thing you never do. I understand this place. The rules of it. The dos and don'ts. I get it. I've had shitty things happen to me. I've lost people. I've…

Get out mate. Get out while you can.

I'm crying.

And her hand comes up to my face and moves my hair out of my eyes.

It's going to be okay. You know that, right? Everything. It all works out in the end.

And I want to ask her how she knows. I want to ask her how she's so sure. I want to tell her about Luke. About Bombhead. Gal… Gal! The race!

What time is it?

SCENE 19

JOANNA: I have just been informed by an *extremely* concerned Mr Bacon, that as the next round involves speaking, and as Princess Dinubolu is Senegalese, the Town Mayor has offered his wife's services as she speaks French.

French? What are you talking about? Don't they speak Senegalian in Senegal?

No – no. Turns out they were colonised by the French, so they speak French.

I don't speak French. And anyway, I've been perfecting my best 'African' accent! Go and tell 'er to go away!

I can't. She's already waiting for you by the mic. Just give it a go, yeah? Good luck.

<u>Good</u>-<u>luck</u>? As in 'good-luck' in spontaneously finding the ability to speak a language fluently??? *(Beat.)* Right.

Silence, s'il vous plaît! Silence! (The crowd are suddenly quiet.) Bonjour et Bienvenue Princesse Dinubolu à Southend!

(Guessing, and speaking in her best French-Essex accent.) Bonjour, Major's Wife.

Dites-nous pourquoi vous aimeriez gagner le vote pour 'Miss Southend'?

Yes????

Je pense qu'elle m'a mal compris, dites-nous pourquoi vous aimeriez gagner le vote pour 'Miss Southend'?

(Picking up on the 'Miss Southend' bit.) Miss Southend? Yes… *(Thinking slowly.)* Erm, would you mind if I spoke in English – I'm trying to practise my best England, you see?

(Surprised.) Oh, oui! Bien sûr!

(Relieved.) Thank you Southend. By voting for me, you would show my people that you are fair to all comers, even if they are chocolate-côloured. *(The audience laugh – they find her rather charming.)*

People have told me that only cream-and-pink English misses can win, and that your judges have no eye for any other sort. I wish to prove them wrong. I feel sure that they will be kind to us all alike. *(The audience 'Aww...')*

People often ask me, how are you so beautiful? Of course I don't want to give away **all** my beauty secrets, but I will tell you one of them...the sand.

Every morning I bury myself up to my neck – you should try it. Nothing makes the skin so velvety. *(The audience laugh and then break into rapturous applause.)*

SCENE 20

FIZA *is still under the bed. It's been a while. Suddenly there's a commotion. Out from under the bed come a pair of Doctor Martens.* **FIZA** *follows.*

FIZA: These are my first pair of Doctor Martens! Can't believe they're still under here.

She puts them on. They don't quite fit.

My feet have shrunk. I'm now two-and-a-half. Used to be a three. That's barely an adult size. Maybe they never fit? Maybe I couldn't stand the idea of feeling like a child forever wearing only kids shoes and forced myself into an adult size?

FIZA *climbs under the bed, pulling out a guitar. It's old and dusty, but you can tell that at some point it was well loved. She cradles it like a baby, looking over every inch of it, tracing her fingers over the strings and picking at the remnants of old stickers.*

A present for my sixteenth birthday. A surprise. I had no idea they were doing that. I can't play. I could never play. But boy did I have fun trying.

She strums a few chords. It's hideously out of tune, but she's happy to enjoy the muscle memory that comes from playing an E minor chord and then a G chord repeatedly – these chords make up the opening to 'About A Girl' by Nirvana. The OTHERS are intrigued, they come out to see what's going on. **FIZA** *encourages them to join her. She hands them instruments, either imaginary, real, or made of cardboard boxes and teaches them to play along with her, the same two chords.*

Look, I'm no performer, yeah, but I certainly had my moments.

*The band switch to playing 'Pretty Fly For A White Guy' by The Offspring. The box glows, it's so happy we've found our way here. **FIZA** laughs, remembering what this song this means to her.*

It is 1999 and The Offspring have released Pretty Fly for a White Guy. My friend group goes mad for it. It's the perfect mix of cheese and catchy lyrics that make an alternative anthem. We decide that for the talent show, we will perform this song.

The OTHERS freak out. There's no way they're going to perform in front of all the cool kids.

I don't have a musical bone in my body, but the others are brilliant so we rely on them to do the heavy lifting.

Emboldened by this revelation they begin to play with great vigour.

A few of us decide to play the girls in bikinis from the music video and act all sexy at the back.

A mic appears. She takes it. Doesn't sing into it, but uses it as an accessory.

The day we perform this song in front of our year group, parents and teachers, The Offspring are number one in the charts. That means that EVERYONE has heard of this song, our song is now *the* song of the moment.

FIZA *and the OTHERS all rock out.*

For three minutes and eight seconds the tables are turned, and the losers that hang out by the radiator messing up the school's one-way system have got people cheering. They're standing on their chairs! For three minutes and eight seconds we are the coolest motherfuckers in all of Upminster. I feel complete.

*A celebration. Party poppers, lights, glitter. **FIZA** sighs, enjoying the feeling of it as the OTHERS start to clean up the stage around her.*

SCENE 21

JOANNA: Listen. The praise, the love. I've won. Hear them calling my name. It tastes…it tastes stale. The air is…damp. I feel…sad. I feel angry – with myself. *(Listening to them.)* That is not **my** name they are calling. It is not me they want. Me – they see.

(To the crowd, speaking as herself.) Stop! Stop. *Please* stop. *(The cheers continue.)* I DON'T KNOW ANY FRENCH! *(Silence.)* Thank you. Thank you. *(She takes a deep breath.)* I'm sorry. I really am sorry Essex, but I need you to know, that it is not me you love but Princess Dinubolu; her story, her money, her crown – because I, *(Correcting herself) she* is everything you want her to be – everything you yourselves are striving to be and spending far too much time worrying over because you're not. Who told you that just because you don't have enough money, a big enough house, aren't the "right" colour, age – that that means you aren't good enough? At what point will you be so tired of playing the game, so tired of being invisible that you decide the only way you will ever be seen is to pretend to be someone else entirely.

When I was six, my friend Henry and I came across a negro woman over by the pier, a short walk from where we are now. She was sat, leaning up against one of the groins – I remember looking at her thinking it was a very silly place to go to sleep. Her clothes had been torn – some of the buttons on her blouse had been ripped off, yet despite all this, I remember looking at her and thinking how beautiful she was; her dark eyes, the sand in her hair; hair which when I touched it felt like **my** hair. To me, she looked like a princess; a real life sleeping beauty.

Henry found two policemen. One asked if the woman was my mother, I said no as my mother died when I was two.

"Christ, aren't they ugly – Negros. If you ask me, whoever did this, did 'er a favour".

I think it's time things changed – don't you? We're all different, but we are Essex, and in Essex we tend to say it as it is, so this is me telling you, each and every one of you – *Know. Your. Worth.* Because until this moment I didn't know mine, and quite frankly it's the most empowering thing I've ever done, and yes, there'll be consequences but I am ready for them, and I hope they are ready for me.

(Pause.) Well, fudge me, I don't think I've ever spoke so much. I guess that's what happens when you're finally allowed to speak. Can I get a glass of water?

SCENE 22

DAISY: They've taken her away. Special care unit. Upstairs. Not even on the same floor. They need to check... god knows what they need to check. Lost half my blood apparently. Nice one Daisy. I could see it on the floor as they wheeled me out. Half covered up with blue paper towel. No wonder they call it theatre coz it's a fucking drama and a half.

A rush as she relives it all. Something goes snap inside.

I could just leave.

Leave her with them. Disappear. Write a note on the back of this Breastfeeding Guide saying "I can't do it. Look after her for me." Run and hide and wait for the milk to dry up. She'll never have to see that half finished lemon bon-bon box room. Never have to know me. Let them find her a mum who knows what she's doing, who won't be a disaster. She'll be better off. House with a garden. Inheritance. Security. One of those ultra sorted couples who've got all that love and the future all planned and only one thing missing.

She is stunned by panic. She searches for an exit. She realises she can't.

SCENE 23

TAG: There is a delicacy to the way she takes the bend. There
shouldn't be. We're easily doing twenty miles over
the speed limit. She accelerates out of the corner and
ratchets through the gears till it no longer feels like we
are connected to the road. We fly me and her.

And she talks.

And I reply.

And she talks some more.

And…

And that's just between us.

That's mine.

And hers.

A perfect moment of wonder.

Fate.

And as we hit the A127 I can see the clock on the dash
of her car turn to one minute past midnight.
And I can feel that knot in my stomach again.
But now it's not about tomorrow.
It's not about Manchester.
University.
Being good enough.
Fitting in.
It's about my mates.
My best mates.
My lie down in front of traffic for me mates.

She drops a gear and the revs shoot up till the needle on
the dial no longer has anywhere to go. Just red. We pass
normal people. In their normal cars. Just driving. *Driving*.
The word can't be the same for what I'm experiencing.
What she's doing. This is more than driving.

And in the distance I can see the flashing blue lights of an ambulance.

I can just about make out the wreckage of a car. Smashed up across the barrier in the central reservation.

I can just make out...

Gal!

And I'm already unbuckling my seat belt. I'm already reaching for the door handle.

I'll be at the Southbound McDonald's at 1.30am.

She kisses me on my cheek. I can feel my jaw slacken. And she just smiles. Smiles that perfect smile. And then she's gone.

By the time my brain restarts I'm already running across the motorway, ignoring the ambulance people waving.
I'm running towards my mates.
My best mates.
My lie down in traffic for me mates.
And Gal goes to say something to me.
But before he can I just grab him.
Throw my arms around him.
And Bombhead looks at me with those sad happy eyes that dogs have.
So I open my arms and he moves towards us.
And we just stand there.
The three of us.

A moment.

Get off me you gay prick.

Gal's the first one to break it. But he's smiling. He knows.

You seen the cowboy?

Bombhead's smiling too. He gestures to the absolute write off that is the Cowboy's Honda Civic, now at one

71

with the central reservation. The cowboy stands with the paramedics looking him over. No lasting damage. Except to his pride. To his status. And that's terminal round here.

Gal had him. Before he spun out. He had him.

I look at Gal. His smile now ear to ear.

It was close.

But you had him. You fucking had him.

Yeah, I di–
We.
We did.
We fucking had him.

I never did get to the McDonalds that night.
So I never did meet Her again.
We just drove home.
Like we always did
And as they dropped me off down my road
We said goodbye like it was just any other night.
Like next weekend we'd be back doing this exact same thing.
And although I saw them again
On random trips home from University
That was the night.
The last night.

Gal finally did get out of his dad's garage though. Signed up to fight a war in a country he couldn't even point out on a map. KIA. An unexploded IED by the side of the road. There's a lot of acronyms in war. I think he'd like that. There were a lot of acronyms in cars too.

His family invited me to his funeral
One of his best mates they said…
I hadn't seen him in seven years.
Too busy.
Too busy doing this.
Too busy pretending.

Bombhead messages me from time to time.
Social media
I don't have his number anymore
Or more pertinently
He doesn't have mine.
Just silly videos.
Memes.
Some provocative
Some slightly racist.
I haven't replied in a year or so.
My best mate.
My lie down in front of traffic for me mate.
My only mate...
Left.

SCENE 24

FIZA *on stage. The large box has been unpacked.*

FIZA: What do you with trauma once it's unpacked? Not saying
that all this is trauma...but some of it is, with a little t.
Some of it has hurt, and I've held onto it for a long time.
Some of it isn't ready to be unleashed just yet.

I think it's okay to not know what to do with it. I think it's
okay to be a work in progress? I am not responsible for
what happened to me.

*She opens the smaller box and a later section of 'This Modern Love' by Bloc Party
pours out.* **FIZA** *listens to it. It hurts.*

But it is my responsibility to come to terms with it.
Maybe not right now though.

There's a type of darkness that some of us are born with.
It ebbs and flows, like waves. Sometimes it crashes onto
rocks, spitting up sea foam and at other times it tickles
your ankles as you calmly stand on the shore.

I was that woman at the top of the cliff. Long hair, straggly
at the ends. I might be again, in the future. I tell you what
though. I will never let myself be a cardigan again.

ALEXA *chimes.*

ALEXA: I'm reminding you –

FIZA: Alexa stop.

ALEXA: I can't. You need to do this.

FIZA: I'm ready to RSVP.

ALEXA: Great, what's your status.

FIZA: Attending.

ALEXA: Confirming two guests.

FIZA: No, just one. Just me.

ALEXA: Confirmed. Have a great day.

FIZA: Alexa, play Celebrity Skin by Hole.

She does.

SCENE 25

We're back with **EUNICE**. **EUNICE** *is sat on a chair out of breath. She's talking to her Head of Year.*

DAISY *curls up, pulls the sheet up over her. She cries. She pulls her phone out, close – it lights her face up – she texts.* **FIZA** *gets a notification on her phone* **DAISY** *falls asleep with the phone in her hand.*

EUNICE: She tried to cut me off!!! I told her I hadn't finished. I bet if I'd have been chatting about something else, something like Anne of Cleves, or pesto, she wouldn't have interrupted. It is true!

      What do you mean '*This isn't like me*'? No, there is nothing going on here at school – I ain't being bullied. No, I'm not depressed! I feel the best I've ever felt in my life! No, there aren't any problems at home – well, actually my brother ate the last of the Pringles last night and…

Sorry for what? Okay, I didn't know Mrs Bates had a bad hip. If she'd have said – Well, how would you react to someone coming at ya? I moved two steps, she two moved steps. I didn't know it was going to turn into a game of 'Cat and Mouse'.

What is that film? That old film with that bloke – he's dead now but was buff! 'Filthy dancer'? *Dirty Dancing!* Thank you! What do I mean? I mean *'Nobody puts Baby in a corner'*. She tried to corner **me**! I didn't ask Mr Taylor and Ms Marsh to join in, did I? Well, do you know how hard it is to try and speak and run and the same time, especially as I'm in Set 3 for PE?

Well shouldn't *she* be sorry to *me* for only allowing us to talk about Black people at school in October? Well, what about the other eleven months of the year? Well, tell her to talk to the government then. How am I being ridiculous?

Where are my role models then? Coz we don't study no one who looks or sounds like me. And the **one** time I find someone, I get told to pipe. Do you know how hard I worked on that? I'm Essex and proud but can't help but feel Essex ain't proud of me. It's in the silence.

Was it *true*? You mean, did I make it up? Some of it, yeah. Why you shouting?! I had to. I had to make some of it up because barely any of it survived. Yeah, well maybe I should. But why should it just be *me*? Ain't we all got a responsibility to find 'em? I think there's loads more out there too. No, they ain't 'hiding'. They were hidden and we should be asking ourselves why. *(Pause.)*

Mrs Bates ain't gonna let me talk again next year is she? But that don't matter. I've a feeling that what happened today is gonna be talked about for a *very* long time…

SCENE 26

Music. Morning.

DAISY: They brought her to me in the middle of the night.

I can't stop staring at her. Familiar as my own body but strange as the moon.

A moment. She plays with her new stomach.

And suddenly – poof – empty.

I can honestly say, now, right, that there is absolutely fuck all that can prepare you for giving birth. Labour is a fucking other-worldly headfuck. Labour really is a lone journey. A one woman odyssey. Solo space trip.

We're so deliberately blind to it all. To mums. To their fragility and strength. Everybody gets born, but nobody wants to bloody hear about it.

We're never tender enough with them. Their bodies. We never hug them as much as they'd like, or lovingly pat the place that was our home for nine months. We don't really think. Just sit there having a cup of tea with her, and just there, under the table, is that silent bit inside her where we grew. Where we started. Where her organs literally moved up into her ribcage to make space for us. We never rub our mums' lower backs and think of all the ongoing aches they've got because of us. Their clicky knees, their tired feet. We don't think of Them Before Us. We think we thank them, and we sort of do on their birthdays or Mothers' Day or with flowers on a Sunday just because, but also – we don't. Not in a dedicated 'I am actually thinking of every tiny thing you've been through to be my mum' sort of way. We couldn't do it if we tried. And they probably wouldn't want the fuss if we could. Because they are just our Mums being our Mums.

I can't wait to have all that.

Footsteps. A curtain is pulled back.

Morning my darling

Morning Mum.

SCENE 27

TAG: The song stops. And so do I. And I'm just stood there in this foreign town. With these people looking at me. These people aren't my friends. These people aren't my people.

Richard?

That's not my name.

Richard.

Tag. That's what my friends call me. Tag Junior.

I'm already turning round and heading towards the door. My neck already being released from that tie that has chained it to a desk for the last ten years. Chained me to this life. And my collar pops up. Just like it always used to. And some cat on the street shouts out

OI OI CANTONA

But I've already passed him. Just a cursory shout of

IRONS

Just cursory

I'M FOREVER BLOWING BUBBLES

And the catboy doesn't understand. He doesn't get it. But it doesn't matter. Not anymore. And my feet start to pick up pace. I'm striding out. I'm running. Sprinting.

And there is that fine rain in the air. The type you always get in this shithole northern town. But it feels apt. It feels like Southend. The Front. On a windy day. With my mates. When I was a kid.

When I was…

The car keys hit the lock. This shitty estate agent car. My car. Not even Bombhead would look twice at this. I slam it into first gear. A cheeky wheel spin. Gal would be proud. And then I'm heading straight to the M6. Southbound.

Fifty miles per hour

Fifty-five

Sixty

Sixty-five

I am the bastard love child of Chas and Dave

Billy Bonds and Bobby Moore

Of illegal raves listening to happy hardcore

Even though it's shite.

Jumping Jacks

China White

Ikon and Diva every Saturday night

Seventy…

Seventy-five…

Eighty…

My father's son.

The product of where I grew

Gal and Bombhead

Me and You…

Luke.

It turns out that getting out weren't all it was cracked up
to be. And all that time you used to talk about. The time
we were wasting. Trapped there. On Colville Close
It turns out…
If I could…
I'd love to waste it again.
I really would mate.
I'd love to waste it again with you.

Eighty-five

Ninety

Ninety-five…

The car is fucking shaking. Shaking like it might just
explode right there on the motorway. But the radio is
playing out some dirty fucking drum and bass. And my
foot won't stop pressing the throttle down. Right down.
And I know. I just know.

Now I know.

One

Hundred

Miles

Per

Hour.

Get the round in lads.

Mine's a Stella.

Home.

Yeah.

I'm coming home…

To the misfits.

The Essex Girls

The fake tan.

The chavs.

The Lager

Lager,

Lager,

Lager.

Shouting

Essex…

My Essex.

Blackout.